A.O.T.K.M.
AMBASSADORS OF THE KINGDOM MINISTRIES

Sharing Purpose and Identity

Preface

For everything that's made, we call it a creation. Every creation made, is proof that there is a creator. Whether we realize it or not, the creator has a specific intent and purpose for his creation. We all at one time or another have acknowledged that we are God's creation, and He is our Creator.

There is not one human being on this planet that was created without purpose. Your life is very valuable to

God and He had a specific purpose for your life when he created you. The goal of this book is to assist the reader in finding their identity and purpose in God's Word. Then and only then, will we experience the life that God truly intended for us. Knowing our purpose will help us to fulfill the will of God and be a blessing to the world and those around us.

Since man's conception he has struggled with the question of his identity and purpose. Who am I? Why did God create me? Why am I here? While the answer has always been before us we continue to seek it everywhere else except the source. In order for us to get the appropriate answers to these questions we must go to the source. If you owned a Mercedes Benz and wanted information or even repairs regarding your vehicle you would contact the manufacturer of the vehicle. Who else would have the finite details concerning how to operate the vehicle and maintain it? How to use all of its features to their full potential, but the one who created it? Who else would know man's purpose, be able to encourage him to his full growth and potential with intimate knowledge of his needs, but God, his Creator. We know that we are created by God, and we are His creations. He has provided the manual for His creation; His word (the Bible). Until we seek the source, we will continue to live unfulfilled lives, never reaching our full potential. It is similar to a new employee starting their job without knowing their job title and description. He or she will find themselves LOST and Confused! In principle, this is exactly what God has stated the problem to be, when He said that my people are destroyed for the lack of knowledge (Hosea 4:6). For this reason, many people are not living to their full potential. God is showing us that what we don't know is hurting us. Our lack of knowledge is destroying our ability to become the best we can. Our Ignorance causes us to be just like that new employee; Lost and Confused.

In many cases, the problem or the difficulty gives an indication of the solution. For example, if I am in someone's home and say that I am thirsty (problem) more likely than not the host would offer me water (solution), Although I did not ask for anything, my host would know that water or a beverage is the solution, even though I only presented my problem, which in many cases is the reciprocal of the solution. If the lack of knowledge is the reason for our destruction, then attaining knowledge and understanding must be the answer for our reconstruction. We are being held captive by the ignorance and lies from the enemy about who we really are. However, God chose to solve the problem Himself. In the Gospel of John (8:31-32) Jesus said "if you abide in My Word you are my disciples indeed. And you shall know the **truth** and the **truth** shall make you **free**". Clearly you can see that the key to your freedom is to increase in knowledge and understanding of who you are. All of these answers can be found in His Word!

He not only told us, but humbled Himself and came to the earth in the flesh (1 Tim. 3:16) to be an example of how mankind is to live on earth. Our Lord Jesus Christ is that example. In Deuteronomy 18:15, Moses told the people "The Lord will raise up for you a Prophet like me from your midst, from your brethren Him you shall hear". In verse 18, the Lord told Moses "I will raise up for them a Prophet like you from among their brethren, and will put My words in His mouth, and He shall speak to them all that I command Him". Our faithful brother Paul said in 1 Corinthians 11:1 "Imitate me, just as I also imitate Christ". The Father Himself told us in Luke 9:35" This is My beloved Son. Hear Him"!

We discussed earlier about the new employee, who started a job without his job title and description. Picture that same employee being introduced to the star employee of the company by the owner. The new employee would see the star employee model the owner's desire concerning his employees and vision of his company through his work ethics and behaviors. We are that new employee and Jesus is the Star Employee that we are to follow. Here are some important points to consider:

> ➤ Jesus is the example for all mankind to follow (1 Peter 2:21, 1 John 2:6).

- He is the Way, the Truth, and the life. No one comes to the Father except through Him (John 14:6).
- The Father God and Moses stressed the importance of the Word He spoke (Luke 9:35, Deut. 18:15, 18-19).
- Paul instructed us to imitate him, only because he imitated Christ.

How can you imitate someone that you are not familiar with? You can't! In order for this to be accomplished, we must study the life of Jesus. First we must learn to think and talk like Him (our job is much easier, because of the Holy Spirit that resides in us). What did Jesus say and talk about? What did He do? By studying the following scriptures in this session you will be able to answer these questions and learn your job description as a follower and Ambassador of Christ.

Matthew 4:17 is Jesus' debut statement. For He said "Repent for the Kingdom of Heaven is at hand"! He was instructing them to change, because the Kingdom had now come. They could no longer do what they were doing and enter the Kingdom of Heaven.

Matthew 4:23 states Jesus went about all Galilee, teaching in their synagogues, preaching the **gospel** of the **kingdom**, and healing all kinds of sickness and all kinds of disease among the people. The word gospel means good news. In this scripture, we see the good news Jesus preached was the Kingdom. For example, my son hears me say that I have a taste for fruit. I provide instructions for him to go to the store to buy me some pineapples. However, he returns with grapes. Although, the fruit he returned with is good, he did not follow my instructions. My request was for a specific fruit; pineapples. Some of us in the church have been guilty of committing this same act of rebellion and still continue to do so, just as my son in the example above. We preach the gospel of prosperity, grace, salvation, healing, and deliverance, but not the gospel of the kingdom. Just as I was specific with the fruit I requested in the example, Jesus was very specific regarding the subject matter of His message.

Matthew 9:35 states, Then Jesus went about all the cities and villages, teaching in their synagogues, preaching the gospel of the kingdom, and healing every sickness and every disease among the people. The bible is very clear on highlighting when Jesus is speaking. Understanding that what He is saying is so important, that many bibles highlight His words in red. We recognize that every red Word in the bible is the words of Jesus. Luke 4:43 states but He said to them, "I **mus**t preach the kingdom of God to the other cities also, because for this **purpose** I have been sent." This is Jesus himself stating what He preached and providing one of the main reasons for His coming. We see this by the use of the word "must", which means required or obligated to. The other word would be "purpose", which means reason, motive, or intentions. Don't take it from me; take it from the source Himself. It's written in RED.

He also instructed, and gave His disciples power and authority to do the same thing. In Luke 9:1-2 it states

Then He called His twelve disciples together and gave them power and authority over all demons, and to cure diseases. He sent them to preach the kingdom of God and to heal the sick.

After Jesus was crucified and resurrected, He showed Himself to the apostles and His message and instructions was still the same. This is shown in Acts 1:3 as it states to whom He also presented Himself alive after His suffering by many infallible proofs, being seen by them during forty days and speaking of the things pertaining to the kingdom of God.

The primary message that we are to preach is the same message that Jesus preached and was first preached by John the Baptist in Matt 3:1-2. Since the time of John the

Baptist this was the message that was to be preached. Luke 16:16 states "The law and the prophets were until John. Since that time the kingdom of God has been preached, and everyone is pressing into it. Showing that before John the Baptist it was the time and era of the law and the prophets, but with John the Baptist and afterwards it's about the gospel of the kingdom. Let me provide you with an illustration of this. Let's say you tell your children they can play video games until 9:00pm, but afterwards they have to clean up. The word until indicates a cut off point and a change in activity. Playing video games was the activity up until 9:00pm, from 9:00pm on, the activity would change to cleaning up. Using our example as an interpretation of the scripture (LK. 16:16), the law and the prophets would represent the activity of playing the game, John and the kingdom of God would represent 9:00pm and the activity of cleaning up.

Jesus first preached the Kingdom in Matthew 4:17after John the Baptist prepared the way and was subsequently thrown into prison. Jesus also instructed His disciples to spread the same message and to teach others to do so as well (Matt 28:19). Phillip preached the same message to the city of Samaria (Acts 8:12). We are aware that Paul wrote the majority of the New Testament and this was his message as well. The following scriptures give us a reference to what Paul preached.

Acts 19:8 And he (Paul) went into the synagogue and spoke boldly for three months, reasoning and persuading concerning the things of the kingdom of God.

Acts 20:25 And indeed, now I know that you all, among whom I have gone preaching the kingdom of God, will see my face no more.

Acts 28:23 So when they had appointed him(Paul) a day, many came to him at his lodging, to whom he explained and solemnly testified of the kingdom of God, persuading them concerning Jesus from both the Law of Moses and the Prophets, from morning till evening.

Acts 28:30-31 Then Paul dwelt two whole years in his own rented house, and received all who came to him, preaching the kingdom of God and teaching the things which concern the Lord Jesus Christ with all confidence, no one forbidding him.

You may be now wondering why it is so important that this is the message that we all <u>should</u> preach. God told us to hear His Son Jesus and He preached it. John the Baptist, The Apostles, Phillip, and Paul also preached this message. The answer to the question is Matthew 24:14. The very End of age is contingent upon it. We now know that we are to preach, teach, and share the Gospel of the Kingdom. The question you may now be asking is "what is the Kingdom"?

When we read the Bible, we see that Jesus' primary subject is the Kingdom of God. He also instructed his followers to preach this same message. However, what exactly is the Kingdom of God. Many people agree that it is the subject matter of the Bible, but do not share the same concept of its meaning. In order to find out its true meaning we must pray and ask God to give us revelation from His Word.

In the beginning God gave mankind dominion over the earth and everything in it. This is clearly stated in Genesis 1:26, Then God said, "Let Us make man in Our image, according to Our likeness; let them have dominion over the fish of the sea, over the birds of the air, and over the cattle, over all the earth and over every creeping thing that creeps on the earth". This was God's motivation for creating mankind. When Adam sinned against God, all of humanity lost what he lost; dominion over the earth. It was always God's will from the beginning to have mankind rule over the earth and it hasn't changed. God is the same yesterday, today, and forevermore (Hebrews 13:8). He desires for man to rule the earth with the government of Heaven. For example, the United Kingdom at one point had dominion over Belize, which is a country in Central America. The United Kingdom would station an Ambassador or governor in Belize to assure that the people were conducting themselves as if they were in the U.K. In the same light God has stationed us (humans) on earth to conduct the affairs of heaven and to produce Kingdom citizens. Many of us are unaware that Heaven is a nation and we are its citizens here on earth. The bible states in Philippians 3:20 for our citizenship is in heaven, from which we also eagerly wait for the Savior, the Lord Jesus Christ. You can only acquire a citizenship from a government of a nation, which in our case is Heaven.

This is why in Psalms 115:16 states; The heaven, even the heavens, are the LORD's; but the earth He has given to the children of men. We are to be Kings on earth and rule it with the government of heaven.

Isaiah 9:6-7 states; For unto us a Child is born. Unto us a Son is given; and the government will be upon His shoulder. And His name will be called Wonderful Counselor, Mighty God, Everlasting Father, Prince of Peace. Of the increase of His government and peace there will be no end.

Isaiah was prophesying about the coming of Jesus. However, Jesus was not coming alone; He was coming with the government of God upon His shoulders delivering it to mankind.

Let's take a look at the beginning of Matthew 6:9-10. This is the prayer Jesus instructed His disciples to pray and how we pray it today with little understanding. It goes;

Our Father in heaven- (We are praying to our Father God and giving His location).

Hallowed be your name- (we are acknowledging that He and His name are holy).

Your kingdom come. Your will be done on earth as it is in heaven. We are requesting that the government of heaven comes to the earth, that the whole earth would reflect heaven.

We have recited this prayer many times and never understood the true revelation of what we are asking for. Praise be to God that this is His will. We still need to understand it, because it is our responsibility to manifest the reality of His super natural government until it becomes our common reality. It was never about a religion, but the government of heaven coming to impact earth through us.

Close your eyes and visualize a picture of what you know about heaven. We know that there isn't any sickness, diseases, or demons in heaven. This is why God gave you power and authority to heal the sick and cast out demons, because in our government sickness and demons are Illegal! When the devil attempted treason in heaven, he was cast out with a third of heaven. God so desires the earth to reflect heaven that He made us in His image and likeness to continue to cast the devil and his demons out. Remember on earth as it is in heaven. This is the job that he gave to mankind.

Jesus preached and demonstrated the kingdom of God by casting out demons, healing the sick and raising the dead. In Matthew 12:28, Jesus says; but if I cast out demons by the Spirit of God, surely the kingdom of God has come upon you.

Jesus is saying when we agree with the Holy Spirit that we are operating in God's government here on earth.

When Adam sinned we not only lost the dominion over the earth, we also lost the indwelling of the Holy Spirit which is the source of God's kingdom.

We thank God for the work that Jesus did. His blood cleansed us so that we once again could receive The Holy Spirit and the power to administrate God's government on the earth. No longer does the Holy Spirit come upon us, but now resides in us. This is why the bible says you are of God, little children, and have overcome them, because <u>He who is in you is greater</u> than he who is in the world (1 John 4:4).

Luke 17:20-21 says;

Now when Jesus was asked by the Pharisees when the kingdom of God would come, He answered them and said, "The kingdom of God does not come with observation; nor will they say, "See here! Or See there! "For indeed, the kingdom of God is within you".

So as we see, the source of God's kingdom is working through you!!!!!!!!

We know what Jesus preached and what He did, we also learned what God's kingdom is, now we begin our life long journey of living in the kingdom of God on earth. There are **three vital principles** to living in the kingdom of God on earth. **These principles are love, faith, and obedience.**

Love is the foundation of how we are to live in the kingdom of heaven on earth.

In Deuteronomy we begin to learn what is expected of us when we make the choice to follow Jesus and live in the kingdom of heaven on earth.

Deuteronomy 6:5 we receive a commandment (instructions) telling us "You shall **love** the Lord your God with all your heart, with all your soul, and with all your strength.

We then receive the second greatest commandment in Leviticus 19:18 that you shall **love** your neighbor as yourself.

God then shares with us how much He loves us in this statement, found in John 3:16

"For God so loved the world that He gave His only begotten Son, that whoever believes in Him should not perish but have everlasting life.

In John 13:34-35, Jesus reaffirms Gods instructions of how imperative love is in the kingdom.

"A new commandment I give to you, that you love one another; as I have loved you, that you also love one another. By this all will know that you are My disciples, if you have love for one another.

Here we learn the keys to living in the kingdom of heaven and we learn the keys to longevity, it is not a cream or a pill, but living according to our Kings decrees (laws) that were established to provide us with the tools needed to live life as promised by Our Father in Heaven.

God makes several promises to us when we choose to surrender our hearts to Him and live in the kingdom. *Romans 8:28 is one example where it states; "and we know that all things work together for good to those who **love** God, to those who are the called according to His purpose".*

Here are a few statements from our constitution (Bible) that teaches us first what faith is and how important it is to live by faith

Faith must work; it must produce; it must be visible. Verbal faith is not enough; mental faith is insufficient. Faith must be there, but it must be more. It must inspire action. Faith endures trails. Trails come and go, but a strong faith will face them head on and develop endurance. Faith understands temptation. It will not allow us to consent to our lust and slide into sin. Faith **obeys the Word. It will not merely hear and not do.** Faith harbors no prejudice. Faith is more than mere words; it is more than knowledge; it is demonstrated by obedience; and it overtly responds to the promises of God. Faith controls the tongue. Faith acts wisely, it gives us the ability to choose wisdom that is heavenly and to shun wisdom that is earthly. Faith produces separation from the world and submission to God. Faith provides us with the ability to resist the Devil and humbly draw near to God. Faith waits patiently for the coming of the Lord. Through trouble and trails faith helps to stifle complaining.

There are many scriptures in the Bible that teach and confirm the importance of faith; the above statement is only a heart opener. Hebrews 11:1 says, but without faith it is impossible to please Him, for he who comes to God must believe that He is, and that He is a rewarder of those who diligently seek Him.

In the Old Testament Habakkuk 2:4 we receive information on living in the kingdom, it states that the just shall live by faith, God establishes for us in His word by telling us that His word will be confirmed by two or three witnesses, this is confirmed in the New Testament in Romans 1:17 and Galatians 3:11.

We learn to love and our faith is strengthened through our obedience to the word of God. Faith produces obedience.

Obedience

One of the most important teachings that God provides to us as His children, is found in these words, "Now it shall come to pass, **if you diligently obey** the voice of the Lord your God, to observe carefully all His commandments which I command you today, that the Lord your God will set you high above all nations of the earth. And all these blessings shall come upon you and overtake you, **because you obey the voice of the Lord your God** (Deuteronomy 28:1-2)". In John 14:15, Jesus says "if you love Me, you will obey my commands". This is how we demonstrate our love to God the Father by being obedient to His word.

We as citizens of the kingdom have a responsibility to love, pray, tell people about Jesus, and to obey God's Word. We must be intentional to seize the opportunity everyday in our homes, communities, work places and schools to demonstrate the will of God. People all around us are looking for answers. They're seeking help for their families, their marriages and physical needs. They're seeking direction for their lives and help in making decisions. And we have been blessed with the answer. The bible says "Heal the sick, cleanse the lepers, raise the dead, cast out demons. Freely you have received; freely give (Matt 10:8)". Today, be a witness to others through the things you say and do. Tell them what Jesus has done in your life, and make sure you are growing in your knowledge of the Word. Draw near to God by developing a more intimate relationship with Him. Serve Him faithfully with the skills and abilities He has given you. Start the work of discipleship, evangelism, and pray for God to raise up mature, spirit-led citizens to advance God's Kingdom.

This is a prayer we can say daily,

Father, use me for Your Kingdom. Help me be ready to witness to others. I commit my time, talent, and treasure to you. Use me to bring the Gospel to the nations. In Jesus name, Amen.

Blessed are the meek, for they shall inherit the earth.

Blessed are those who hunger and thirst for righteousness, for they shall be filled.

Blessed are the peacemakers, for they shall be called sons of God

You are the light of the world, Let your light shine before men, that they may see your good works and glorify your Father in heaven.

Other Books by A.O.T.K.M.

CITIZENSHIP

The purpose of this book is to introduce you to your rights as children of God and citizens of His government; The Kingdom. Our purpose is to avoid the complexity of religious myths and to simplify the revelation of your rights as citizens of this awesome and wonderful government.

Fred Hates Red

Walk with Fred as he learns about the importance of having a relationship with God, the power of prayer, color combinations, and that God created us all to love and not hate.

We want to hear from you!

To learn more about AOTKM, you can visit our website at www.aotkm.org. You can also send us an email at info@aotkm.org. We would love to hear from you. Let everything that has breath praise the LORD! (PSALMS 150:6)

Made in the USA
Monee, IL
10 February 2025